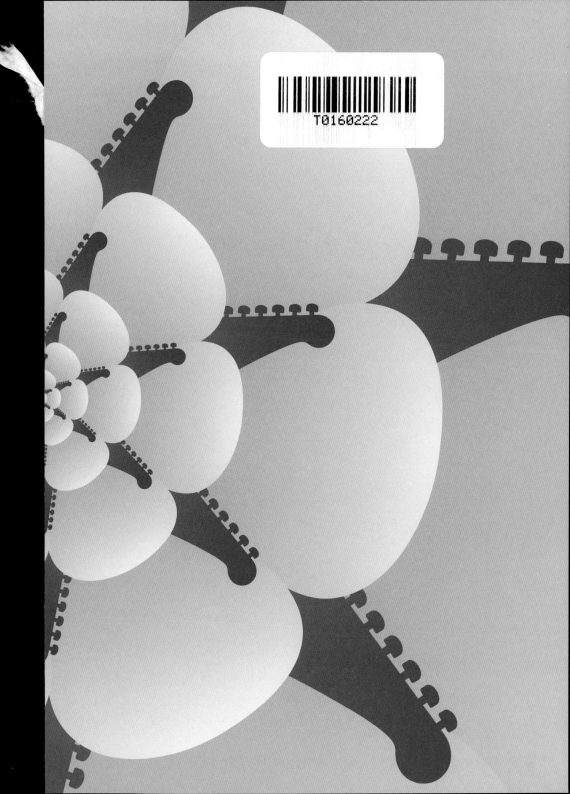

BIOGRAPHIC
HENDRIX

BIOGRAPHIC
HENDRIX

LIZ FLAVELL

AMMONITE
PRESS

First published 2018 by
Ammonite Press
an imprint of Guild of Master Craftsman Publications Ltd
Castle Place, 166 High Street, Lewes, East Sussex, BN7 1XU,
United Kingdom
www.ammonitepress.com

ISBN 978 1 78145 315 5

A catalogue record for this book is available from the
British Library.

Publisher: Jason Hook
Concept Design: Matt Carr
Design & Illustration: Matt Carr & Robin Shields
Editor: Jamie Pumfrey

Colour reproduction by GMC Reprographics
Printed and bound in China

CONTENTS

ICONOGRAPHIC   06

INTRODUCTION   08

01: LIFE   11

02: WORLD   35

03: WORK   53

04: LEGACY   75

BIOGRAPHIES   92

INDEX   94

ICONOGRAPHIC

WHEN WE CAN RECOGNIZE A MUSICIAN BY A SET OF ICONS, WE CAN ALSO RECOGNIZE HOW COMPLETELY THAT ARTIST AND THEIR MUSIC HAVE ENTERED OUR CULTURE AND OUR CONSCIOUSNESS.

INTRODUCTION

There are certain people who seem to live their lives at the perfect time, to inhabit their moment on the planet so fully that they come to define it. It is almost impossible to think of the end of the Swinging Sixties – of Carnaby Street, Woodstock and the Isle of Wight Festival – without immediately conjuring the image of Jimi Hendrix. If this was a time of revolution – sexual, cultural, racial and political – then Hendrix was its bandmaster. Hendrix's lifestyle and lyrics spoke of the new sense of freedom and desire for sensory 'experience'; his fashions forged the template for the modern rock star; and, fundamentally, his extraordinary guitar-playing created the soundtrack for a generation. His untimely death also symbolized the end of the revolution, fusing forever the link between the man and his time.

Hendrix was a founding member of the '27 Club' of musicians, who dazzled briefly but brilliantly before dying at the tragically young age of 27. But in his short time in the spotlight, he transformed the art of the electric guitar to such a degree that he is still widely regarded as the greatest rock guitarist of all time. His mastery of distortion and feedback, along with his sexualized stagecraft, mean that nearly 50 years later guitarists still can't hip-thrust their guitar, crank up a wah-wah or dive-bomb a tremolo arm without summoning Hendrix's head-banded, psychedelic ghost. And beneath it all was such a fluid, virtuoso mastery of blues and jazz chords and riffs that guitarists born long after he died still begin their education with Hendrix's take on 'Hey Joe'.

Johnny Allen Hendrix was born in 1942 in Seattle, Washington, to Lucille and Al Hendrix – his father changed his son's name to James Marshall Hendrix a few years later. His mother was an alcoholic, and from the age of nine Jimi was cared for by a strict father with strong religious beliefs. When Lucille died, the teenage Hendrix sought solace in poetry, painting and playing the guitar. He discovered the blues, and Muddy Waters, Elmore James and Howlin' Wolf became his idols.

After some teenage delinquency and an inglorious stint in the 101st Airborne Division, a discharge from the army granted Hendrix a lucky escape from the Vietnam War. In 1962, he took to the road as a jobbing guitarist, touring across the USA. In the South, old blues guys taught him tricks like playing the guitar behind his back and with his teeth. Finding work with the backing bands for Sam Cooke, Jackie Wilson, B.B. King, The Isley Brothers and Little Richard, he perfected his licks.

"HIS RIFFS WERE A PRE-METAL FUNK BULLDOZER, AND HIS LEAD LINES WERE AN ELECTRIC LSD TRIP DOWN TO THE CROSSROADS, WHERE HE PIMP-SLAPPED THE DEVIL."

—Tom Morello, *Rolling Stone*, 2015

By 1966, Hendrix was in New York with his own band, Jimmy James and the Blue Flames. Chas Chandler of The Animals saw him play in Greenwich Village and invited him to come to the UK. London in 1966 was a hip, swinging place, with British bands like The Beatles, The Rolling Stones, Cream, and The Who playing small clubs. But when Hendrix took to the stage, even such legendary players as Eric Clapton and Brian Jones were blown away. The following year, Hendrix recorded the ground-breaking album *Are You Experienced* and the single 'Purple Haze', while also famously setting fire to his guitar at the Monterey Pop Festival.

Hendrix had less than five years of mainstream success, culminating in legendary performances at Woodstock in 1969 and the Isle of Wight in 1970. He became hugely famous through mesmerizing performances, laconic television interviews and fantastic fashions: military jackets, feathered fedoras and psychedelic scarfs acquired from groupies all weaving into the legend. And then, on 18 September 1970, it was all over.

To use infographics to explore the life, world, work and legacy of such a free spirit might seem counter-intuitive. And yet, in the numbers, timelines and statistics iconic imagery of the infographics perhaps we can capture something of what made Hendrix such a man of his moment: the 5 years of music, the 6 strings of his signature chord, the legendary run of 47 gigs in 54 days, the 37 different electric guitars and the crowd of 700,000 that turned up to see their hero at the Isle of Wight Festival in 1970.

"IT'S FUNNY THE WAY PEOPLE LOVE THE DEAD. YOU HAVE TO DIE BEFORE THEY THINK YOU ARE WORTH ANYTHING. ONCE YOU ARE DEAD, YOU ARE MADE FOR LIFE."

—Jimi Hendrix, *Starting at Zero, His Own Story*, 2013

JIMI
HENDRIX

01
LIFE

"IT'S THE MOST PSYCHEDELIC EXPERIENCE I EVER HAD, GOING TO SEE HENDRIX PLAY. WHEN HE STARTED TO PLAY, SOMETHING CHANGED: COLOURS CHANGED, EVERYTHING CHANGED. THE SOUND CHANGED ..."

"... I REMEMBER FLAMES AND WATER DRIPPING OUT OF THE ENDS OF HIS HANDS. I REMEMBER HIM PLAYING ... AND DOING SOMETHING WITH HIS TONGUE AND THINGS HAPPENING AROUND HIM IN THE AIR. HE WAS SUCH A MANIPULATOR, SUCH A MAGICIAN TO ME."

—Pete Townshend of The Who, *Crosstown Traffic: Jimi Hendrix and Post-war Pop*, 2012

UNITED STATES OF

◀ Also from Washington:
Kurt Cobain (1967–94),
singer and guitarist
of Nirvana

JAMES MARSHALL HENDRIX

was born on 27 November 1942 in Seattle, Washington, USA

AMERICA

Jimi Hendrix was born Johnny Allen Hendrix at Seattle's King County Hospital. His mother Lucille struggled with alcoholism and ill health, and his father Al was in the army and spent long periods away – a combination that meant Jimi was often cared for by friends and relatives. In 1945, Al was honourably discharged from the army. After collecting Jimi from a family friend in California, Al returned to Seattle and promptly changed his son's name to James Marshall Hendrix.

USA

James Petrillo, leader of the American Federation of Musicians, orders a strike against record companies for withholding royalties. No musician is allowed to produce any commercial recording, but live performance is encouraged. The ban is not lifted until 1944.

USA

Capitol Records is founded by Johnny Mercer with financial backing from Buddy DeSylva and Glenn Wallichs.

USA

The musical film *Star Spangled Rhythm* is released to boost morale during the Second World War.

THE MUSIC WORLD IN 1942

While war dominated the world stage, what was happening on the music scene?

FRANCE

André Coeuroy publishes *Histoire Générale du Jazz (General History of Jazz)*.

UNITED KINGDOM

Bomb damage to the Queen's Hall means that The Proms are relocated to the Royal Albert Hall.

Composers John Ireland, Granville Bantock, Arnold Bax and Benjamin Britten deliver a letter to the wife of the Soviet Ambassador, sending greetings to their Soviet counterparts as a symbol of peace and diplomacy during the Second World War.

SOVIET UNION

Shostakovich's 'Leningrad Symphony No. 7 in C Major, Op. 60' is given its world premiere and broadcast across the Soviet Union.

GERMANY

Public and private dance events are prohibited by the Nazis.

ON THE JUKEBOX

**VERA LYNN
GLENN MILLER
JIMMY DORSEY
DUKE ELLINGTON
BENNY GOODMAN
FRANK SINATRA**

ROCK 'N' ROLL BABY BOOM

GRAHAM NASH
2 February

BRIAN JONES
28 February

LOU REED
2 March

ARETHA FRANKLIN
25 March

IAN DURY
12 May

19

PAUL McCARTNEY
18 June

BRIAN WILSON
20 June

CURTIS MAYFIELD
3 June

JERRY GARCIA
1 August

JIMI
HENDRIX
27 November

ISAAC HAYES
20 August

THE HENDRIX FAMILY TREE

GRANDMOTHER

Zenora Moore
(1883–1984)

GRANDFATHER

**Bertran Philander
Ross Hendrix**
(1866–1934)

FATHER

**James Allen 'Al'
Ross Hendrix**
(1919–2002)

SISTER

**Pamela Marguerite
Hendrix**
(b. 1951)

BROTHER

**Joseph Allen
Hendrix**
(b. 1949)

SISTER

**Kathy Ira
Hendrix**
(b. 1950)

BROTHER

**Alfred
Hendrix**
(b. 1953)

In 1941, Al Hendrix met Lucille Jeter at a dance in Seattle. The couple were married in March 1942, just three days before Al was due to join up with the armed forces in Oklahoma. Eight months later, Jimi was born. Al returned from his three years of service in 1945 and finally saw his son for the first time.

Al and Lucille attempted to save their failing marriage, having another son, Leon, followed by four other children who were later put into care. By 1951, they were divorced and Al was awarded full custody of Jimi, Leon and Joseph. Lucille moved north to Canada and remarried.

GRANDFATHER

Preston M Jeter
(1875–1943)

GRANDMOTHER

Clarice Lawson
(1892–1967)

RIX

MOTHER

Lucille Jeter
(1925–58)

BROTHER

**Leon Morris
Hendrix**
(b. 1948)

Jimi Hendrix
(1942–70)

DAUGHTER

Tamika Laurice James
(b. 1967)
Born in California to
Diana Carpenter. In 1970,
just a few days before
Jimi's death, lawyers for
both parties met to
discuss paternity.

SON

**James Henrik
Daniel Sundquist**
(b. 1969)
Born in Sweden to
Eva Sundquist.

YOUNG JIMI

1947

Jimi's parents' constant arguing makes him nervous. He suffers from a stammer and dreams up an imaginary friend called Sessa. He also gets his first instrument – a harmonica.

1958

In February, Jimi's mother, Lucille, dies.

1959

Al buys Jimi his first electric guitar – a white Supro Ozark 1560 S.

1960

Jimi drops out of high school at the age of 17. He starts a band, playing rock 'n' roll songs. At their first gig, they earn 35 cents each.

1951

Al and Lucille divorce and Jimi is raised by his father who works as a gardener. Money is tight and Al, a military man, cuts Jimi's hair so close to his head that he is called 'Slick Bean' at school.

1955

At school, Jimi shows a talent for art. He often visits his grandmother in Vancouver, where he watches TV and listens to the radio. He becomes hooked on the songs of Chuck Berry and Muddy Waters and their "real primitive guitar sound".

1956

Jimi buys his first acoustic guitar for $5 from a family friend. The right-handed guitar is rather beaten up and has only one string.

1961

Jimi is caught riding in a stolen car and is given a two-year suspended sentence. He enlists with the 101st Airborne Division and, during a parachute jump, Jimi breaks his ankle and injures his back.

1962

After 14 months in the army, Jimi is discharged due to behavioural problems. Heading to a local bar with a paycheck for $400, he manages to spend most of it, leaving with less than $20. Jimi decides to hit the road to make a living from music ...

MUSICAL HIGHWAY

"A rolling stone gathers no moss" and nor did Hendrix In the years between 1962 and 1966, as he travelled around the USA playing music. Staying in more than 100 different places and backing dozens of artists gave Hendrix an entirely unique education.

SOUTH

Hendrix kicks off by playing guitar in the streets, in cafés and in bars. It doesn't earn him much so he starts a band called The King Kasuals with Billy Cox, a friend from the army. The Kasuals tour Tennessee, Kentucky, Arkansas and Indiana.

SOUTH

Hendrix on the audiences in the South:

"DOWN THERE YOU HAVE TO PLAY WITH YOUR TEETH OR ELSE YOU GET SHOT!"

NASHVILLE

Hendrix moves into an unfinished housing development – the house he occupies has no floor or roof.

Hendrix joins Solomon Burke, but is later traded to the band of Otis Redding in exchange for two horn players. After less than a week, Hendrix is fired due to his onstage antics.

NEW YORK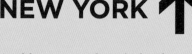

Hendrix competes in and wins the 'Amateur Night' contest at the Apollo Theater. He struggles to find work and sleeps rough. In 1964, he briefly joins The Isley Brothers on tour, and records the song 'Testify'.

Hendrix joins Curtis Knight & The Squires, but finds it hard:

"I JUST GOT TIRED, MAN ... I WANTED MY OWN SCENE, MAKING MY OWN MUSIC ... I WAS STARTING TO SEE THAT YOU COULD CREATE A WHOLE NEW WORLD WITH AN ELECTRIC GUITAR."

Hendrix takes a turn in the backing bands of Sam Cooke, Jackie Wilson, B.B. King and Chuck Jackson.

ATLANTA

Hendrix joins Little Richard's backing band. Little Richard runs a tight ship and Hendrix is often berated for his appearance. They part company after six months and Hendrix rejoins The Isley Brothers.

HARLEM

In 1966, Hendrix starts his first serious band – the Blue Flames. The group attracts the attention of record labels such as Epic and CBS. English model Linda Keith persuades Chas Chandler, bassist of The Animals, to come and see the band play. He is so impressed he offers Hendrix a ticket to England ...

"HE BROUGHT HIS OWN GUITAR. HE WAS LEFT-HANDED BUT THIS WAS A NORMAL RIGHT-HANDED GUITAR AND SO EVERYTHING WAS UPSIDE DOWN. HE PLAYED JUST ABOUT EVERY STYLE YOU COULD THINK OF, AND NOT IN A FLASHY WAY. HE DID A FEW OF HIS TRICKS. PLAYING IT BEHIND HIS HEAD AND WITH HIS TEETH. I THINK WE DID JUST THAT SONG ['KILLING FLOOR']. THEN HE WALKED OFF AND MY LIFE WAS NEVER THE SAME AGAIN."

—Eric Clapton, remembering the first night he played with Hendrix

WELCOME TO LONDON!

In the early hours of 24 September 1966, Hendrix arrived at Heathrow Airport, London. He was 23 years old and was carrying just a small holdall of belongings. Without a proper work permit, Hendrix was kept waiting at the airport for four hours before finally being issued a seven-day travel visa. During an action-packed first week in London, Hendrix jammed with Zoot Money and Andy Summers (later of The Police), and met Kathy Etchingham and The Animals.

WHAT HENDRIX BROUGHT TO ENGLAND ...

1 x small holdall with 1 x change of clothes

1 x new Burberry raincoat

1 x jar of face cream for his acne

1 x set of hair rollers

1 x Bob Dylan songbook

1 x guitar – it had to be carried through customs by one of his management team as Hendrix didn't have a work permit.

RIDING HIGH

By October 1966, with the addition of Noel Redding on bass and Mitch Mitchell on drums, Jimi had his own band – The Jimi Hendrix Experience. The following year the trio hit the road and 1967 would turn out to be quite a ride!

Are You Experienced reaches Number 2 in the UK.

Jimi sets fire to his guitar at the Monterey Pop Festival, California.

'The Wind Cries Mary' is released in the UK. In June, it rises to Number 6.

Are You Experienced is released in the UK.

'Purple Haze' is released in the UK. In May, it peaks at Number 3.

'Hey Joe' reaches Number 6 in the UK.

'Hey Joe' is released in the USA, but fails to chart.

JUL

JUN

MAY

APR

MAR

FEB

JAN

AUG

SEP

OCT

NOV

DEC

'Burning of the Midnight Lamp' climbs to Number 18 in the UK chart.

The Jimi Hendrix Experience's second album *Axis: Bold As Love* is released in the UK.

'Foxy Lady'/'Hey Joe' peaks at Number 67 in the USA.

Hendrix is voted 'Pop Musician of the Year' by the readers of *Melody Maker*.

Are You Experienced is released in the USA, where it eventually peaks at Number 5.

'Purple Haze'/'The Wind Cries Mary' reaches Number 65 in the USA.

THE REAL JIMI

HUMOUR

5
4   6
3   7
2   8
1   9
0   10

SHYNESS

5
4   6
3   7
2   8
1   9
0   10

Hendrix enjoyed telling shaggy dog stories – he'd make sure he got his victim believing his tale and then say "woof, woof" to let them know they'd been had – he called this "selling a woof ticket". When things got tense in the recording studio, Hendrix would play 'Teddy Bears' Picnic' to lighten the mood.

Hendrix was often described as introverted. When he was young he had a stutter, but the confidence he gained from playing the guitar helped him overcome that problem. Bobby Womack remembered:

"JIMI WOULD COME INTO A ROOM AND, AS BIG AS HE WAS, HE'D JUST EASE OVER INTO A CORNER AND SIT DOWN AND JUST SAY 'HEY MAN, WHISPER WHISPER' LIKE HE WAS AFRAID TO TALK."

Hendrix lacked confidence about his voice: "I just wish I could sing really nice. But I know I can't sing. I just feel the words out. I just try all right to hit a pretty note, but it's hard. I'm more of an entertainer and performer than a singer."

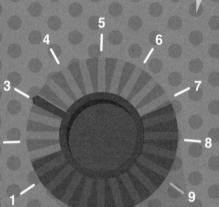

CONFIDENCE

TEMPER

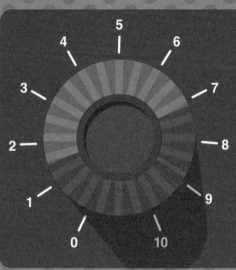

ESCAPISM

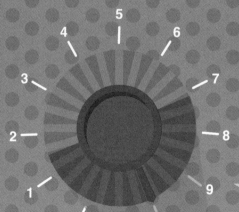

Hendrix's mood changed quickly when he drank alcohol. Drink had made Al Hendrix violent and Jimi was no different. He regularly lashed out at people and smashed up hotel rooms when he hit the bottle.

Hendrix was all about escapism and release – which he found through music, women, drugs and alcohol.

ANATOMY OF A ROCK STAR

RIGHT HAND

Hendrix originally learned to play the guitar right-handed because his father believed being left-handed was the sign of the devil. He ate, wrote and held the telephone with his right hand.

HEIGHT:

According to army records

5 feet 10 inches (1.78 m)

CM

68 69 70 71

WAIST
28 inches
(71 cm)

WEIGHT
11 stone
(70 kg)

HEAD

Hendrix's hats and Afro hair added to the illusion of height.

EYES

Hendrix had poor eyesight, but he refused to wear glasses.

A L
LALO
NGTH
EWATC
HTOWER
HEYJOE
PURPLE
HAZE

FACE

Hendrix's pockmarked face was the result of years of acne. His complexion got worse from his many addictions, too.

LEFT WRIST

The scar on Hendrix's left wrist was from when he tried to slash his wrists some time in New York before he was famous.

LEFT HAND

It wasn't until Hendrix turned his right-handed guitars upside down to play left-handed that things began to rock. He combed his hair, smoked and threw with his left hand, too.

THUMB

Hendrix's thumb was so large that he could stretch the top joint across all six strings.

THE DEATH OF HENDRIX

The final days of Hendrix's life were marred by his insomnia. In his last photographs, taken the day before he died, Hendrix looked tired as he posed with his guitar and a pot of tea in the gardens of the Samarkand Hotel, London. Despite his weariness, he spent the rest of the day shopping and the evening at a party. He was at the peak of his career and no-one could have predicted that his life would be cut short.

FRIDAY, 18 SEPTEMBER 1970

 At 1.45am, girlfriend Monika Dannemann drives Hendrix to a party hosted by Pete Kameron.

 Hendrix leaves the party at 3am and Dannemann drives him back to the Samarkand Hotel. Dannemann makes tuna sandwiches but Hendrix can't sleep and asks her for sleeping tablets, which she refuses to give him.

 The emergency services arrive at 11.27am.

 At 11.18am, Dannemann finds Hendrix unresponsive and calls an ambulance.

 Attempts to resuscitate Hendrix fail and he is pronounced dead at St Mary Abbot's Hospital in Kensington at 12.45pm.

DEATH CERTIFICATE

AGE OF DECEASED:

27

DATE OF DEATH:

Eighteenth September 1970

CAUSE OF DEATH:

Inhalation of vomit.

Barbiturate intoxication

(quinalbarbitone)

Insufficient evidence

of circumstances

OPEN VERDICT

JIMI
HENDRIX

02
WORLD

"WHEN THERE ARE VAST CHANGES IN THE WAY THE WORLD GOES, IT'S USUALLY SOMETHING LIKE ART AND MUSIC THAT CHANGE IT. MUSIC IS GOING TO CHANGE THE WORLD NEXT TIME. YOU SEE, MUSIC DOESN'T LIE. I AGREE IT CAN BE MISINTERPRETED, BUT IT DOESN'T LIE."

—Jimi Hendrix, *Starting at Zero, His Own Story*, 2013

INFLUENCES ON JIMI

CHEROKEE

Hendrix's paternal grandmother was part-Cherokee and taught him the history of Native Americans. Hendrix liked to wear the shawls and ponchos that she made for him.

THE GRAND OLE OPRY

Hendrix would listen to the country-music show on the radio each week. He was drawn in by the songs of Hank Williams, Roy Acuff and a young Elvis Presley.

MUSIC

Hendrix listened to Muddy Waters, Elmore James, Howlin' Wolf and Ray Charles. He was also a fan of Dean Martin.

POETRY & PAINTING

Hendrix was a shy child, but found poetry was an outlet for his emotions. At school he enjoyed art and would draw pictures of cars, even sending some of his designs to the Ford Motor Company.

ANIMALS

Gentle and quiet, Hendrix loved animals and regularly brought stray dogs home. One time his father allowed a dog to stay – they named it 'Dawg'.

SPACE

Space travel fascinated Hendrix and inspired his own paintings Summer Afternoon on Venus and Valleys of Neptune.

NOTTING HILL

8

JIMI'S SWINGING LONDON

The Jimi Hendrix Experience exploded onto the London club scene in the winter of 1966. Swinging London was the landscape for Hendrix's electric performances and rock 'n' roll lifestyle, but it also became the scene of his untimely death.

 concert   social   home   hotel

4

KENSINGTON

2

6

1 Scotch of St James, 13 Masons Yard
On his first night in London, Hendrix visited this club and asked if he could jam. It was his first time on a UK stage.

2 Blaises Club, 121 Queen's Gate
Hendrix played this basement club just before Christmas 1966. In the audience were Pete Townshend and Jeff Beck.

3 The Ship, 116 Wardour Street
This pub in Soho is where Hendrix, The Beatles and Keith Moon of The Who came to play. Keith Moon was later barred from the pub for letting off a smoke bomb.

4 Royal Albert Hall, Kensington Gore
The Jimi Hendrix Experience played this famous venue a few times, but most notably on 18 and 24 February 1969.

5 23 Brook Street
Hendrix's first real home was shared with his girlfriend Kathy Etchingham. The house next door had been the home of the composer Handel in the 1700s.

6 11 Gunterstone Road
When Hendrix first arrived in London in September 1966, the first place he stayed was in West Kensington, at the home of Zoot Money. Here he jammed with Andy Summers of The Police.

HENDRIX

40

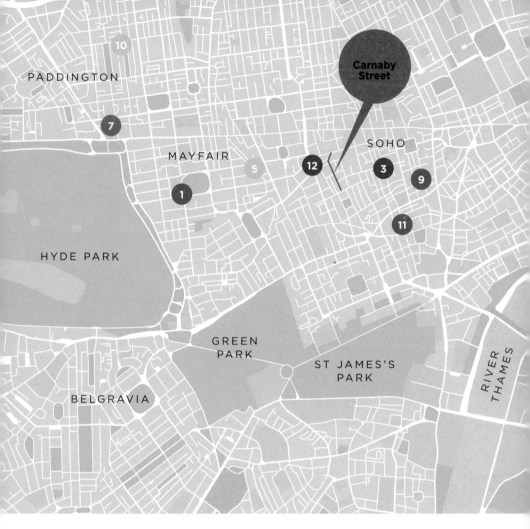

7 **The Cumberland Hotel, Great Cumberland Place**
The Cumberland was one of Hendrix's favourite hotels.

8 **Samarkand Hotel, Lansdowne Crescent**
Jimi was found unresponsive in room 507 of this hotel on the morning of 18 September 1970.

9 **Ronnie Scott's Jazz Club, 47 Frith Street**
Hendrix's final live performance was at this famous jazz club. During an impromptu jam session, he played with Eric Burdon of The Animals.

10 **34 Montagu Square**
Hendrix and Etchingham rented this flat from Ringo Starr in December 1966. The couple lived with Hendrix's manager Chas Chandler and his girlfriend Lotta.

11 **Flamingo Club, 33 Wardour Street**
In February 1967, Hendrix played this Soho club famous for its jazz and R&B music.

12 **The Speakeasy Club, 48 Margaret Street**
Hendrix played here in February 1967 and tried to chat up Mick Jagger's girlfriend, singer Marianne Faithfull. It became one of his favourite clubs.

"THE SWINGING CITY"

—Time magazine, 15 April 1966

CITY OF WESTMINSTER
CARNABY ST.
W 1

Hendrix bought one of his famous military jackets from the 'I Was Lord Kitchener's Valet' on Carnaby Street. Similar jackets were worn by Eric Clapton and Mick Jagger.

I was
LORD KITCHENER'S
Valet

LADY

Barry Gibb of The Bee Gees collected the John Stephen Award for best-dressed male of 1966.

Henry Moss publicized the opening of 'Lady Jane' at 29 Carnaby Street by having girls changing in the shop windows.

Carnaby St. customers included Marc Bolan, Mick Jagger and The Beatles.

In 1966, The Kinks released 'Dedicated Follower of Fashion'.

1966

The American *Time* magazine sang the praises of London and dedicated an entire issue to the place in 1966. The British capital encapsulated the spirit of the age and that was down to its vibrant youth culture. Carnaby Street was the epicentre of the fashion scene, the place where any dedicated follower of fashion wanted to be ...

Twiggy was just 16 years old and weighed 6½ stone (41 kg) when she was the face of fashion.

John Stephen, known as the 'King of Carnaby Street', owned at least 15 boutiques on Carnaby Street and is commemorated with a blue plaque.

JANE

TOMCAT

Hendrix lived around the corner from Carnaby Street in Brook Street.

37 GUINEAS (£38.85) – COST OF A SUIT IN 1966

In 1966, Tom Jones walked along Carnaby Street with Christine Spooner and a cheetah to promote his new 'Tom Cat' boutique.

JIMI HENDRIX

 1 Position in *Rolling Stone's*

ALBUMS
3

LIVE ALBUMS
3

SINGLES
14

> "I LIKE THE WAY ERIC CLAPTON PLAYS. HIS SOLOS SOUND JUST LIKE ALBERT KING."

1992
Year inducted into the Rock & Roll Hall of Fame

FAVOURITE GUITAR:
'Black Beauty' – a black 1968 Fender Stratocaster. Hendrix last played the guitar live at the Isle of Wight Festival in August 1970. Nobody knows where the guitar is today but its serial number is 222625.

YEARS ACTIVE
1962 – 70

BORN
1942

2

ERIC CLAPTON

SINGLES
67

LIVE ALBUMS
14

ALBUMS
23

FAVOURITE GUITAR:
'Blackie' – built in 1970 from the parts of three 1950s' Fender Stratocasters and finished in black. Clapton used the guitar in the studio and on stage between 1974 and 1984. 'Blackie' was auctioned off in 2004 for $959,500.

"[JIMI] IS REALLY ONE OF THE FINEST MUSICIANS AROUND."

2000
Year inducted into the Rock & Roll Hall of Fame

YEARS ACTIVE
1962 –

BORN
1945

WORLD

LEGENDARY LOOKS

Hendrix changed the face of male fashion when he arrived in London in the 1960s. At the time, bands such as The Rolling Stones and The Beatles were kitted out in made-to-measure suits, but Hendrix's military jackets and use of jewellery inspired many to follow in his fashion footsteps.

SCARVES AND BANDANAS

Scarves were a staple of Hendrix's wardrobe, and in 1968 he began tying them around his arms and legs for dramatic effect. As his career progressed, he swapped his hats for bandanas.

MILITARY MAN

One of Hendrix's first looks was that of a Bohemian army officer. This vintage military jacket was acquired from the famous 'Granny Takes a Trip' boutique on Kings Road, Chelsea.

SILK SHIRTS

Hendrix shopped at the Portobello and Kensington markets, picking up fancy dress shirts. At the Monterey Pop Festival in 1967, Hendrix wore this yellow silk shirt, designed by Mick Jagger's brother, Chris Jagger.

VELVET COWBOY

Hendrix picked up this wide-brimmed Westerner-brand cowboy hat in 1967, and customized it with a purple band and brooches. The hat was stolen in 1968 – many of his clothes were pilfered by fans who wanted to prove they had spent the night with Hendrix.

WOODSTOCK

Fashion designers Michael Braun and Toni Ackerman met Hendrix in 1968 and they designed his Woodstock outfit, as well as all the colourful, billowing shirts for which Jimi became famous.

KIMONOS

Michael Braun and Toni Ackerman were also responsible for many of Hendrix's kimonos. Hendrix loved the soft material, which allowed him full movement of his arms when playing guitar.

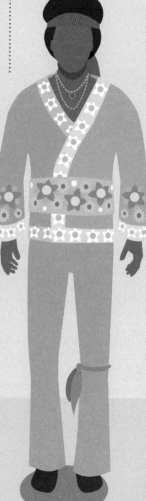

HENDRIX AND THE LAW

Before joining the army in 1961, Hendrix had to declare any record of juvenile delinquency on his application. The statement he gave revealed a previous incident when Hendrix and a friend were caught stealing clothes. It was the first in a long line of run-ins with authority.

IN THE ARMY NOW

Hendrix never seemed to be the right fit for military life and his discharge form shows a string of incidents that led to his dismissal. He may have told people that his departure was due to medical issues, but the truth was a little more revealing:

> "Behaviour problems, requires supervision while on duty, little regard for regulations, apprehended masturbating in platoon area while supposed to be on detail."

$80

Debt owed for laundry services. Hendrix said he'd given the money to a friend, but was later found to be lying.

5 Number of servicemen who gave written statements on Hendrix's bad behaviour.

3 Number of times Hendrix was punished for missing bed check.

1961

In May, Hendrix was arrested while joyriding with friends. Two weeks later, he was arrested again for the same crime. At his trial, the judge gave Hendrix two options: a two-year jail sentence or the punishment suspended if he joined the army.

1962

Hendrix was arrested at a civil rights demonstration in Nashville.

1968

In a Stockholm hotel room, Hendrix broke a window and injured his hand in a drug-and-booze filled fury. After being charged with criminal damage, local authorities placed Hendrix under a travel ban, forcing him to report to the police station every day for two weeks.

1967

While playing five nights at the Ambassador Theater in Washington D.C., Hendrix and two friends were arrested for jaywalking.

1969

Hendrix was arrested at Toronto Pearson International Airport for the illegal possession of narcotics. He was later released on a $10,000 bail.

SOUNDS NOISY

Jimi loved to play his music loud. With his stack of Marshall amps – levels dialled to 10 – he created deafening sounds. How loud Jimi played is unknown as his performances were never recorded in decibels, but from eyewitness accounts and live footage we know it was a serious volume. In 1972, two years after Hendrix's death, the Guinness World Records began monitoring the situation when Deep Purple registered 117 dB at a London gig. So how loud is loud and who's the loudest?

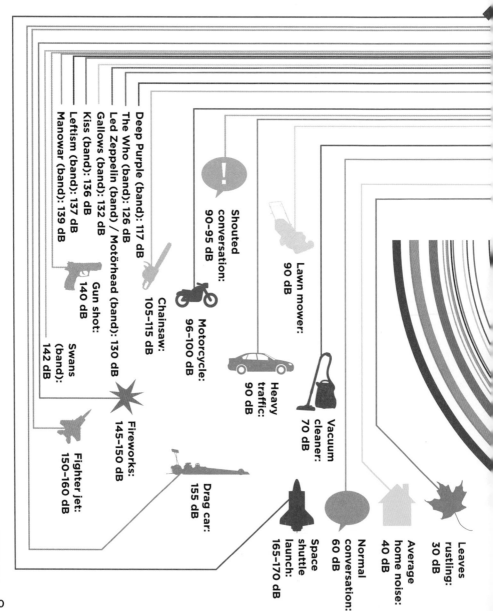

Manowar (band): 139 dB

Leftism (band): 137 dB

Kiss (band): 136 dB

Gallows (band): 132 dB

Led Zeppelin (band) / Motörhead (band): 130 dB

The Who (band): 126 dB

Deep Purple (band): 117 dB

Shouted conversation: 90–95 dB

Lawn mower: 90 dB

Chainsaw: 105–115 dB

Motorcycle: 96–100 dB

Gun shot: 140 dB

Swans (band): 142 dB

Heavy traffic: 90 dB

Fireworks: 145–150 dB

Fighter jet: 150–160 dB

Drag car: 155 dB

Space shuttle launch: 165–170 dB

Vacuum cleaner: 70 dB

Normal conversation: 60 dB

Average home noise: 40 dB

Leaves rustling: 30 dB

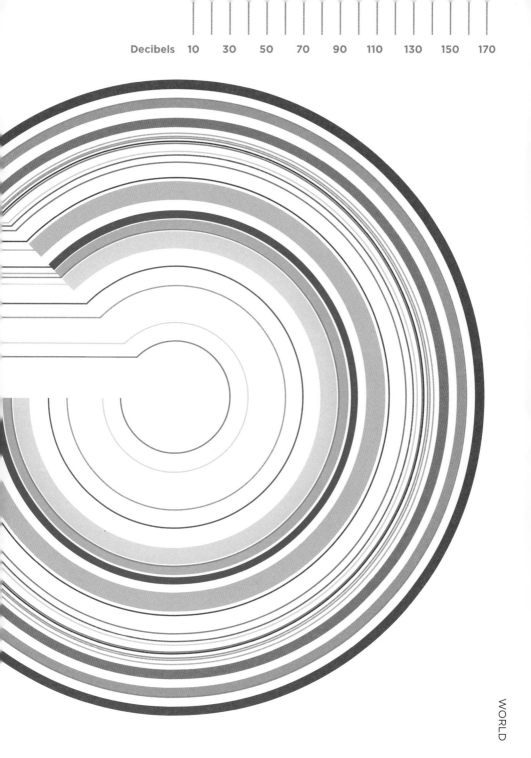

5 LEFT-HANDED GUITARISTS

PAUL McCARTNEY
(THE BEATLES / WINGS)

KURT COBAIN
(NIRVANA)

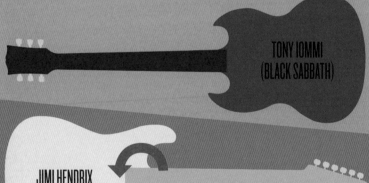

TONY IOMMI
(BLACK SABBATH)

JIMI HENDRIX

ALBERT KING
(BLUES GUITARIST)

JIMI
HENDRIX

03
WORK

"JIMI BROKE SO MUCH GROUND BY LOOKING AT THE GUITAR AS AN INSTRUMENT OF EXPRESSION AS OPPOSED TO SOMETHING THAT JUST MAKES A SOUND. HE LIVED THROUGH HIS GUITAR. YOU COULD HEAR IT SING, YOU COULD HEAR IT CRY AND YOU COULD HEAR IT LAUGH. HE EVEN MADE IT SOUND LIKE A MACHINE GUN ..."

—Huey Morgan of Fun Lovin' Criminals,
Rebel Heroes, 2015

ANATOMY OF AN ALBUM:

ARE YOU EXPERIENCED
1967

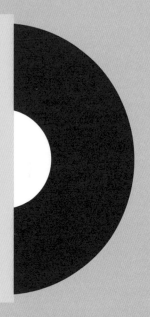

Hendrix hated the UK album artwork. The USA cover was more to Hendrix's taste and features the band at London's Kew Gardens, photographed through a fish-eye lens.

The Jimi Hendrix Experience had been together only a few weeks before they recorded 'Hey Joe', which would be included on the US release of *Are You Experienced*. Money was tight and time in the studio was expensive so the band didn't have time to mess around – for that reason many of the songs were created in the studio and recorded in only one take. "Imagination is the key to my lyrics, and the rest is painted with a little science fiction," explained Hendrix. Roger Mayer, who built Hendrix's guitar pedals, likened the sound of the guitars "to taking someone on a space journey". The result is a psychedelic masterpiece that divided critics at the time, but is now revered as one of rock's finest moments.

HIGHEST CHART POSITION:

USA
5

UK
2

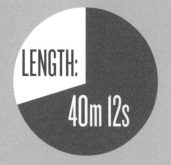

LENGTH:
40m 12s

RECORDED:
OCTOBER 1966 TO APRIL 1967

RELEASED:
UK: 12 MAY 1967
USA: 23 AUGUST 1967

THE PLAYERS

JIMI HENDRIX

NOEL REDDING

MITCH MITCHELL

THE BREAKAWAYS
('Hey Joe')

PRODUCER: Chas Chandler

SOUND ENGINEERS: David Siddle, Eddie Kramer and Mike Ross

3 ALBUM FACTS

1. The album was recorded over 16 sessions across three studios in London.

2. 'The Wind Cries Mary' was recorded in 20 minutes at the end of one session, but only included on the USA version which also featured the UK singles 'Hey Joe' and 'Purple Haze'.

3. Hendrix lacked confidence as a singer and hated anyone watching him sing, so a privacy barrier between him and the control room was constructed at Olympic Studios.

TRACK LISTING FOR UK & INTERNATIONAL EDITIONS

01 FOXY LADY

02 MANIC DEPRESSION

03 RED HOUSE

04 CAN YOU SEE ME

05 LOVE OR CONFUSION

06 I DON'T LIVE TODAY

07 MAY THIS BE LOVE

08 FIRE

09 3RD STONE FROM THE SUN

10 REMEMBER

11 ARE YOU EXPERIENCED?

THEMES

- Love
- Lost love
- Desire
- Space exploration
- Existential questions
- Soul searching/ Depression
- Drugs

JIMI PLAYS GUITAR

Hendrix was left-handed, but he could play a guitar either way and opted for mostly right-handed models. With the guitar turned upside-down and the strings reversed, the tone of the guitar was affected and added to Hendrix's unique sound. Over the course of his short musical career, he is known to have owned at least 37 electric guitars.

GUITARS

01 1957 Supro Ozark 1560 S
02 1960s Danelectro Bronze Standard
03 1961 Epiphone Wilshire
04 1960s Fender Duo-Sonic
05 1959–64 Fender Jazzmaster
06 1950s/60s Fender Duo-Sonic
07 1964–66 Fender Jazzmaster
08 1960s Fender Stratocaster
09 1964 Fender Stratocaster
10 1960s Fender Stratocaster
11 1966/67 Fender Stratocaster
12 1963 Fender Stratocaster
13 1965 Fender Stratocaster
14 1960s Fender Stratocaster
15 1963/64 Fender Stratocaster
16 1964/65 Fender Stratocaster
17 1965/66 Fender Stratocaster
18 1966/67 Fender Stratocaster
19 1967 Fender Stratocaster
20 1967 Gibson Flying V

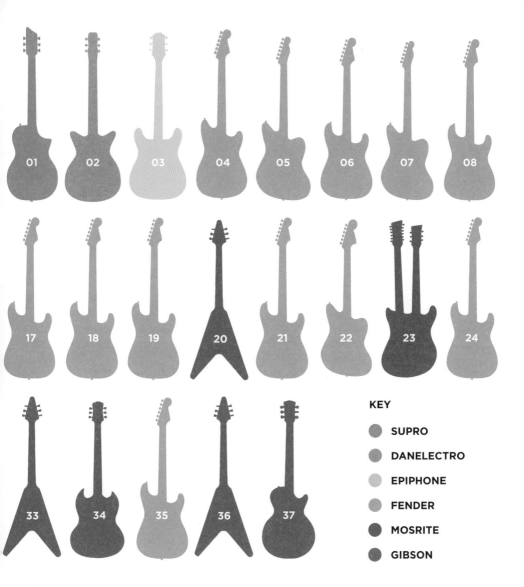

KEY

- SUPRO
- DANELECTRO
- EPIPHONE
- FENDER
- MOSRITE
- GIBSON

21 **1960–64 Fender Stratocaster**
22 **1960s Fender Jaguar**
23 **Mosrite Joe Maphis 12/6 Doubleneck**
24 **1967 Fender Stratocaster**
25 **1965 Fender Jazzmaster**
26 **1956 Gibson Les Paul Custom**
27 **1950s Gibson Les Paul TV Special**
28 **1967/68 Fender Stratocaster**
29 **1968 Fender Stratocaster**
30 **1968 Fender Stratocaster**

31 **1967 Gibson SG Custom**
32 **1960s Fender Stratocaster (with Telecaster neck)**
33 **1969 Gibson Flying V**
34 **1960s Gibson SG Custom**
35 **1968/69 Fender Stratocaster**
36 **1970 Gibson Flying V (left-handed)**
37 **1955 Gibson Les Paul Custom**

LIVE ACTION HERO

LAST UK PERFORMANCE

16 September 1970
Ronnie Scott's Jazz
Club, London

217

NUMBER OF GIGS PERFORMED

RECORD RUN
47 **GIGS** 54 **DAYS**

EARNINGS IN THE EARLY DAYS

In 1967, The Jimi Hendrix Experience
was earning £1,000 a night. The
money was split between the band
members and their managers
Mike Jeffery and Chas Chandler.

$750

$7,500

$18,000

BIG BUCKS

The Jimi Hendrix Experience was earning $70,000 a night by 1968. One show at Madison Square Garden netted the band $105,000.

1967
$1,000
PER NIGHT

1968
$70,000
PER NIGHT

BIGGEST FEE

At Woodstock, Hendrix was paid $18,000 (about $115,000 today) – the highest fee for any performer at the festival. Janis Joplin received $7,500 and Santana $750.

JIMI HENDRIX
£500

MITCH MITCHELL
£125

NOEL REDDING
£125

CHAS CHANDLER
£125

MIKE JEFFERY
£125

WORK

ANATOMY OF AN ALBUM:

AXIS: BOLD AS LOVE
1967/68

Jimi was disappointed with the album artwork. He wanted something that reflected his Native American heritage, but it ended up as a psychedelic portrait of Hendrix as the Hindu god Vishnu.

Hendrix's second recording is less rebellious and has a softer vibe than his first. In Hendrix's own words: "In *Axis* there are more gentle things, more things for people to think about if they want to. It's quieter as far as guitar is concerned, but then we're emphasizing the words." Hendrix enlisted the help of guitar pedal creator Roger Mayer to turn the ideas in his head into real sounds. Together they created the Experience's most innovative music yet, in which Hendrix's guitar playing was enhanced by wah-wah wizardry and studio magic.

HIGHEST CHART POSITION:

USA
3

UK
5

RECORDED:
MAY 1967 TO OCTOBER 1967

RELEASED:
UK: 1 DECEMBER 1967
USA: 15 JANUARY 1968

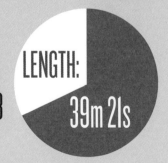

LENGTH:
39m 21s

THE PLAYERS

JIMI HENDRIX

NOEL REDDING

MITCH MITCHELL

ROY WOOD
('You Got Me Floatin'')

TREVOR BURTON
('You Got Me Floatin'')

PRODUCER:
Chas Chandler

SOUND ENGINEER:
Eddie Kramer

3 ALBUM FACTS

1. Hendrix explained the album's title as being about love: "It can turn your whole world upside down, like the axis of the earth. It's that powerful, that bold. People kill themselves for love."

2. Hendrix accidentally left the master tapes of the first side in a taxi. The final version had to be mixed again in a single night.

3. Jimi found the glockenspiel used on 'Little Wing' in the studio next door and instinctively added it to the mix.

TRACK LISTING

01 **EXP**

02 **UP FROM THE SKIES**

03 **SPANISH CASTLE MAGIC**

04 **WAIT UNTIL TOMORROW**

05 **AIN'T NO TELLING**

06 **LITTLE WING**

07 **IF 6 WAS 9**

08 **YOU GOT ME FLOATIN'**

09 **CASTLES MADE OF SAND**

10 **SHE'S SO FINE**

11 **ONE RAINY WISH**

12 **LITTLE MISS LOVER**

13 **BOLD AS LOVE**

THEMES

- Love
- Desire
- Space
- Trip to groovy places/Drugs
- Life stories
- Defiance/ Freedom
- Earth

ELECTRIC BLUES AND OTHER COLOURS

Hendrix had a thing for colour. The full spectrum permeates his music and in his song 'Love or Confusion' he even wondered why there were so many colours without a name. Hendrix referenced almost every hue on the colour wheel in his lyrics ...

RED

'The Wind Cries Mary'
'Red House'
'Crosstown Traffic'
'Spanish Castle Magic'
'Bold as Love'
'1983... (A Merman I Should Turn to Be)'
'House Burning Down'

ROSE

'One Rainy Wish'

ORANGE

'Bold as Love'

BROWN

'Spanish Castle Magic'

YELLOW

'Bold as Love'

GOLD

'Are You Experienced?'
'Wait Until Tomorrow'
'Castles Made of Sand'
'One Rainy Wish'
'Come On (Part 1)'
'Valleys of Neptune'

BLACK
'House Burning Down'

GREEN
'Crosstown Traffic'
'3rd Stone from the Sun'
'Castles Made of Sand'
'Bold as Love'
'Valleys of Neptune'

SILVER
'3rd Stone from the Sun'
'1983... (A Merman I Should
Turn to Be)'
'Angel'

BLUE
'The Wind Cries Mary'
'Remember'
'One Rainy Wish'
'Bold as Love'
'1983... (A Merman I Should
Turn to Be)'
'Valleys of Neptune'
'In from the Storm'

PURPLE
'Purple Haze'
'Bold as Love'
'Valleys of Neptune'

LILAC
'One Rainy Wish'

Hendrix was a key part of the festival scene in the 1960s and 1970. He was a huge hit at Monterey Pop Festival and a wonder at Woodstock, but by the time of the Isle of Wight Festival many thought his star was fading. The crowd of 600,000 that crammed in to see their hero disagreed.

woodstock

• NEW YORK 15–18 AUGUST 1969 •

$7 DAY TICKET PRICE

$18 WEEKEND TICKET PRICE

9 am Time when Hendrix goes on stage. He is the last act on the fourth day.

200,000 EXPECTED ATTENDEES

400,000–700,000 ACTUAL ATTENDEES

2 DEATHS

2 BIRTHS

JIMI PLAYS **2** HOUR SET

HENDRIX'S FEE: **$18,000**

ISLE OF WIGHT

FESTIVAL

• 26–31 AUGUST 1970 •

150,000
EXPECTED ATTENDEES

600,000–700,000
ACTUAL ATTENDEES

1 1/2 YEARS SINCE HENDRIX'S LAST UK APPEARANCE

IT IS HENDRIX'S FINAL MAJOR PERFORMANCE. HE DIES LESS THAN A MONTH LATER.

POPULATION OF ISLE OF WIGHT
100,000

Set list includes a rendition of
'GOD SAVE THE QUEEN'

ANATOMY OF AN ALBUM:

ELECTRIC LADYLAND 1968

Once again, Hendrix disliked the UK cover artwork. He wanted a photograph of the band to be taken by Linda Eastman (later Linda McCartney) but Polydor instead photographed a group of 19 women in the nude, something Hendrix found distasteful.

Hendrix's third and final album is a double – and it is packed with classic tracks. Hendrix summed up this melting pot of far-out visions and imaginative sounds best: "It's slightly electric funk every once in a while, and it goes into the complete opposite on some songs, complete fantasy." This was Hendrix's first outing as producer and it would be his only Number 1 album in the USA.

3 ALBUM FACTS

1. "Electric ladies" was the term that Hendrix used for his groupies.

2. Hendrix never liked the sound of his own voice, but on this album he allowed his vocals to be higher in the mix because he felt he was singing with real feeling.

3. There is confusion over the title of the final track, 'Voodoo Child (Slight Return)'. In the album notes that Hendrix sent to the record company, he listed the songs as 'Voodoo Chile' and 'Voodoo Child (Slight Return)', but when the album was released in the UK, the songs were listed as 'Voodoo Chile' and 'Voodoo Chile (Slight Return)'. Later album reissues follow Hendrix's original spelling.

RECORDED:
JULY AND DECEMBER 1967 & JANUARY, APRIL AND AUGUST 1968

RELEASED:
UK & USA: 16 OCTOBER 1968

HIGHEST CHART POSITION:

USA **1** UK **6**

LENGTH:

75m 47s

TRACK LISTING

01 AND THE GODS MADE LOVE

02 HAVE YOU EVER BEEN (TO ELECTRIC LADYLAND)

03 CROSSTOWN TRAFFIC

04 VOODOO CHILE

05 LITTLE MISS STRANGE

06 LONG HOT SUMMER NIGHT

07 COME ON (PART I)

08 GYPSY EYES

09 BURNING OF THE MIDNIGHT LAMP

10 RAINY DAY, DREAM AWAY

11 1983... (A MERMAN I SHOULD TURN TO BE)

12 MOON, TURN THE TIDES... GENTLY GENTLY AWAY

13 STILL RAINING, STILL DREAMING

14 HOUSE BURNING DOWN

15 ALL ALONG THE WATCHTOWER

16 VOODOO CHILD (SLIGHT RETURN)

THEMES

- Love
- Defiance/ Power
- Life
- Dream fantasy

The album was recorded at Olympic Studios, London; Record Plant Studios, New York; and Mayfair Studios, New York.

THE PLAYERS

JIMI HENDRIX

NOEL REDDING

MITCH MITCHELL

BRIAN JONES ('All Along the Watchtower')

JACK CASADY ('Voodoo Chile')

STEVE WINWOOD ('Voodoo Chile')

PRODUCER: Jimi Hendrix   **SOUND ENGINEERS:** Eddie Kramer and Gary Kellgren

WORK

69

TOURING THE WORLD

Hendrix played with The Jimi Hendrix Experience from October 1966 to June 1969, in which time the band toured Europe and the United States extensively. Life on the road was exhausting – as a result, the band split and Jimi went on to form Band of Gypsys in 1969.

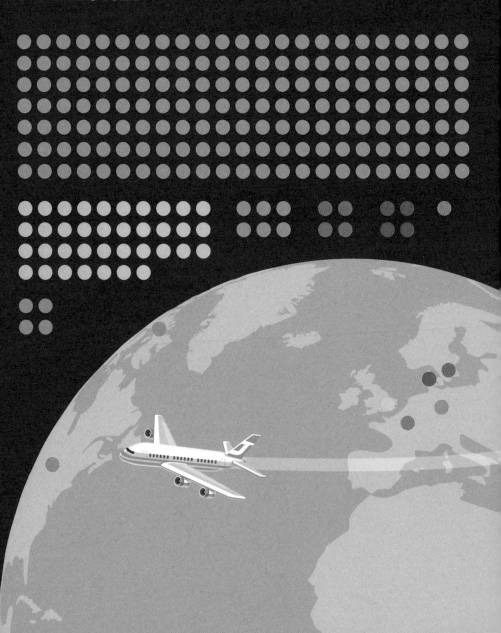

CONCERTS

USA
161

UK
37

GERMANY
6

CANADA
4

SWEDEN
4

DENMARK
4

FRANCE
1

TOTAL
217

MEMORABLE PERFORMANCES

ADMIT ONE | OLYMPIA THEATRE | PARIS | OCTOBER | 1966

MONTEREY POP FESTIVAL | JUNE 1967

★ MARCH 1968 ★ | CAFE AU GO GO | NEW YORK

WINTERLAND BALLROOM | OCTOBER 1968 | SAN FRANCISCO

ADMIT ONE | WOODSTOCK | AUGUST 1969 | • NEW YORK •

ROYAL ALBERT HALL | FEBRUARY 1969 | • LONDON •

FILLMORE EAST | JANUARY 1970 | • NEW YORK • | WITH BAND OF GYPSYS

BERKELEY COMMUNITY THEATER | MAY 1970 | CALIFORNIA

L. A. FORUM | • APRIL 1970 •

• ATLANTA • | INTERNATIONAL POP FESTIVAL | JULY 1970

ISLE OF WIGHT | AUGUST 1970 | FESTIVAL

ANIMAL MAGIC

Hendrix's childhood love of animals is evident in many of his lyrics. The dreamscape of 'Little Wing' is populated with zebras and butterflies, and his songs often referenced the animals he cared for, with even jellyfish and catfish getting a mention.

DUCK
'Rainy Day, Dream Away'

BLUEBIRD
'Valleys of Neptune'

CAT
'My Friend'

HORSE
'House Burning Down'

ROBIN
'She's So Fine'

STARFISH
'1983... (A Merman I Should Turn to Be)'

DOG
'We Gotta Live Together'
'Stone Free'
'My Friend'

MOCKINGBIRD
'Remember'

BUTTERFLY

'Little Wing'
'The Stars That Play with Laughing Sam's Dice'

HONEYBEE

'Remember'

FOX

'Foxy Lady'

JELLYFISH

'Little Wing'
'Message to Love'

ZEBRA

'Little Wing'

DRAGONFLY

'Spanish Castle Magic'

WILDCAT

'All Along the Watchtower'

HEN

'3rd Stone from the Sun'

CATFISH

'Catfish Blues'

THE HENDRIX CHORD

Hendrix combined R&B, funk, blues, rock and psychedelia to great effect. He worked hard at mastering his art and was rarely found without a guitar in his hands, learning new techniques and experimenting with different inversions of chords. He made one chord, E7 (#9), so much his signature that it is often called the Hendrix chord.

E7 (#9)

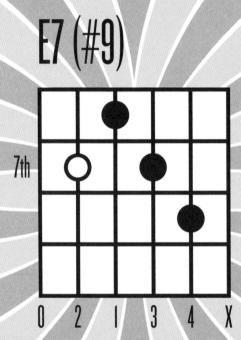

7th

0 2 1 3 4 X

- Hendrix used the chord on 'Purple Haze' – it was more commonly associated with jazz musicians until Hendrix made it his own.

- The dirty, funky, crunchy rock sound in 'Foxy Lady' was achieved using the chord. It was also used on 'Spanish Castle Magic'.

- Hendrix was able to play an impressive array of chords because of his large hands and his ability to play a note on the sixth string with his thumb.

- Single-note riffs are another Hendrix speciality. Songs such as 'If 6 was 9' and 'Voodoo Chile' involve tricky syncopations made possible through muting, slurs, trills and bends.

JIMI
HENDRIX

04
LEGACY

JimiHendrix

DECEMBER 2015

SIMPLY THE BEST

"IT'S IMPOSSIBLE TO THINK OF WHAT JIMI WOULD BE DOING NOW; HE SEEMED LIKE A PRETTY MERCURIAL CHARACTER. WOULD HE BE AN ELDER STATESMAN OF ROCK? WOULD HE BE SIR JIMI HENDRIX? OR WOULD HE BE DOING SOME RESIDENCY OFF THE VEGAS STRIP? THE GOOD NEWS IS HIS LEGACY IS ASSURED AS THE GREATEST GUITAR PLAYER OF ALL TIME."

—Tom Morello, *Rolling Stone: 100 Greatest Guitarists*, December 2015

SOUND CIRCUIT

Hendrix's guitar abilities were legendary, but his style was enhanced by innovative equipment with which he was only too happy to experiment. He travelled with a box of gadgets, sound-effect pedals and spare parts for his guitars, and on stage he controlled everything himself. Hendrix's attention to detail enabled him to create a unique and iconic sound.

WAH-WAH PEDAL 01

The psychedelic sound of the 1960s was down to a new invention called the wah-wah pedal. The distinctive crying sound it made was favoured by Frank Zappa, who introduced Eric Clapton and Hendrix to its sonic possibilities.

By the time The Jimi Hendrix Experience recorded their third album, Hendrix had mastered the wah-wah pedal and used it for the intro to 'Voodoo Chile'.

ROGER MAYER OCTAVIA 02

In 1967, Hendrix became the first musician to try the Octavia pedal when he used it for the recording of 'Purple Haze'. Invented by Roger Mayer, it added an octave overtone to each original note played.

UNI-VIBE PEDAL 04

The Uni-Vibe was a Japanese invention, and created a phase-shifting effect. The song 'Machine Gun' owed much to Uni-Vibe.

FUZZ FACE PEDAL 03

In 1965, there were just four guitar pedals on offer – tape delay, tremolo, spring reverb and distortion. The Fuzz Face, created in 1966 in England, was a simple and cheap distortion pedal. Hendrix used the pedal throughout the recording of *Are You Experienced*.

STRINGS & PICKS

Hendrix used Fender Rock 'N' Roll strings. The gauges would run .010, .013, .015, .026, .032 and .038. He used medium picks.

MARSHALL AMP 05

Both Pete Townshend and Eric Clapton were fans of Marshall amps. Hendrix spoke to both guitarists before he visited Jim Marshall's shop in Hanwell, London, in mid-October 1966. He walked away with three 100W stacks. Hendrix put the new amps to good use when The Jimi Hendrix Experience recorded 'Hey Joe'. In 1967, Hendrix signed a contract with Sunn amps, but after burning them out by playing too loud, he reverted back to Marshall.

AN EXPLOSIVE INFLUENCE

1960s

In London, Hendrix caught the attention of British musicians such as Eric Clapton of Cream, Eric Burdon of The Animals, and Paul McCartney and John Lennon of The Beatles. Brian Jones and Mick Jagger of The Rolling Stones were inspired and before the decade was out, even Hendrix's idol Bob Dylan was a devotee.

2010s

He may be long gone but Hendrix's influence lives on. Josh Homme of Queens of the Stone Age grew up listening to the Hendrix back catalogue. Simon Neil of Biffy Clyro, Josh Klinghoffer of the Red Hot Chili Peppers and just about anyone who picks up a guitar to play has a little Hendrix running through their veins.

2000s

John Mayer proclaimed: "Jimi Hendrix is one of those extraordinary hubs of music where everybody lands at some point. Every musician passes through Hendrix International Airport." Jack White, Tom Morello of Rage Against the Machine and Dan Auerbach of The Black Keys have all alighted at this airport at some time.

"I LISTENED TO HENDRIX FIRST AND TO ME HENDRIX IS THE ULTIMATE GUITAR PLAYER."

—Josh Homme, *Noisey*, 2013

1970s

Even after his death, Hendrix influenced the next generation of guitarists such as Stevie Ray Vaughan. Joe Satriani claimed "my roots were really based on Jimi Hendrix and his style of playing". Meanwhile, Neil Young discovered: "Guitar – you can play it or transcend it. Jimi showed me that."

"HENDRIX THREW A MOLOTOV COCKTAIL ONTO ROCK 'N' ROLL."

—Neil Young, at Jimi Hendrix's induction to the Rock & Roll Hall of Fame, 1992

1980s

In the 1980s, it was Johnny Marr of The Smiths, Robert Smith of The Cure, Yngwie Malmsteen and Steve Vai that were influenced by the music of Hendrix. Lenny Kravitz was a fanatic, too: "You could feel the fire, you could feel the blues. You could feel the sadness. It's unbelievable."

1990s

Hendrix's legacy burned bright through Slash of Guns N' Roses, John Frusciante of the Red Hot Chili Peppers and blues guitarist Kenny Wayne Shepherd.

"WHAT CHANGED MY LIFE WAS THE FREEDOM, THE EXPRESSION THAT HE BROUGHT TO THE PERFORMANCE. THERE WAS A SENSE OF WILD, RECKLESS DANGER."

—Matt Bellamy, *NME*, 5 January 2008

LEGACY

HENDRIX IN NUMBERS

Jimi was the backing guitarist on

24

recordings before he became famous.
....

FIRST RECORDING

THE ISLEY BROTHERS 'TESTIFY'

FIRST TV APPEARANCE

In 1965, Jimi performed in the backline for Buddy and Stacy performing 'Shotgun' on Nashville's Channel 5 show *Night Train*.

THE JIMI HENDRIX EXPERIENCE

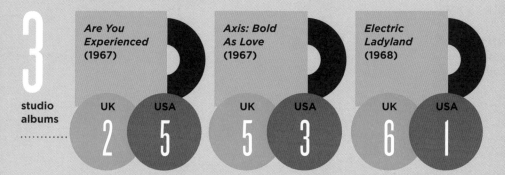

3 studio albums

Are You Experienced (1967)
UK **2** USA **5**

Axis: Bold As Love (1967)
UK **5** USA **3**

Electric Ladyland (1968)
UK **6** USA **1**

14 singles

HIGHEST SELLING SINGLE:

'All Along the Watchtower'

UK **5** USA **20**

BAND OF GYPSYS

1 live album

Band of Gypsys (1970)
UK **6** USA **5**

'NEW' MATERIAL

On 1 March 2013, *People, Hell and Angels,* a 12-track album of Hendrix songs recorded between 1968 and 1969, was released. Many of these songs were planned for Hendrix's intended next album, *First Rays of the New Rising Sun*.

1 single

'Stepping Stone' (USA)

The (2

JIMI HENDRIX
(1942–70)

JIM MORRISON (1943–71)
KURT COBAIN (1967–94)
RICHEY EDWARDS, MANIC STREET PREACHERS (1967–95)
DAVE ALEXANDER, THE STOOGES (1947–75)

PETE HAM, BADFINGER (1947–75)
ALAN WILSON, CANNED HEAT (1943–70)
CHRIS BELL, BIG STAR (1951–78)
D. BOON, MINUTEMEN (1958–85)

7 Club

JANIS JOPLIN
(1943–70)

BRIAN JONES (1942–69)
AMY WINEHOUSE (1983–2011)
RON 'PIGPEN' MCKERNAN, GRATEFUL DEAD (1945–73)
ROBERT JOHNSON (1911–38)

PETE DE FREITAS, ECHO & THE BUNNYMEN (1961–89)
KRISTEN PFAFF, HOLE (1967–94)
RANDY "STRETCH" WALKER (1968–95)
MIA ZAPATA, THE GITS (1965–93)

THE HENDRIX HOUSE

In July 1968, Hendrix moved into the small upstairs flat at 23 Brook Street with his girlfriend Kathy Etchingham. During his time in London, Hendrix lodged with friends and stayed in hotels, but he described Brook Street as his real home.

Two centuries earlier, composer George Frideric Handel had lived in the house next door, at 25 Brook Street. Handel leased the entire building when it was considered to be a modest town house. Hendrix was inspired by his neighbour of yesteryear and would spend hours listening to classical music.

In 2016, the flat was opened as a museum, with Etchingham helping to recreate the rooms in which they lived.

4
Number of months that Hendrix lived at 23 Brook Street.

£30
Rent paid each week.

3pm
Time the couple got out of bed in the afternoon. They would often stay up until 5am to jam with fellow musicians, including George Harrison and Eddy Grant.

Jimi wrote the riff for 'All Along the Watchtower' in the flat.

HANDEL LIVED AT 25 BROOK STREET FOR AROUND 40 YEARS

OXFORD STREET

NEW BOND STREET

SOUTH MOLTON ST.

BROOK STREET

DAVIES ST.

BROOK'S MEWS

GROSVENOR ST.

The central location meant that Handel was near to Covent Garden Theatre, St James's Palace and the King's Theatre in Haymarket where he regularly performed.

80
Number of pieces of fine art in the home.

£60
Rent paid each year for the entire house.

74
Age Handel was when he died in his bedroom at the house in 1759.

LEGACY

AXIS: BOLD AS LOVE LITTLE WING FENDER STRATOCASTER WAH WAH VOODOO FUZZ

COVERING HENDRIX

It takes guts to cover the works or the songs made famous by arguably the best guitarist ever. 'Hey Joe' and 'All Along the Watchtower' were not Hendrix originals, but he made them his own. Which artists have dared to copy Hendrix?

TOP 10 COVERED SONGS

1 **'PURPLE HAZE'**
Covered by: The Cure, Ozzy Osbourne, Frank Zappa, The Stooges, Soft Cell

2 **'LITTLE WING'**
Covered by: Stevie Ray Vaughan, Sting, The Corrs, Derek and The Dominos

3 **'FOXY LADY'**
Covered by: Cee-Lo Green, The Cure, Booker T and The MGs

4 **'FIRE'**
Covered by: Red Hot Chili Peppers, Alice Cooper

5 **'MANIC DEPRESSION'**
Covered by: Jeff Beck with Seal, Elephant Tree

6 'THE WIND CRIES MARY'
Covered by: John Mayer, Richie Sambora, Jamie Cullum, Sting, Seal

7 'VOODOO CHILD (SLIGHT RETURN)'
Covered by: Stevie Ray Vaughan, Yngwie Malmsteen, Kenny Wayne Shepherd

8 'CROSSTOWN TRAFFIC'
Covered by: Living Colour, Dave Grohl

9 'RED HOUSE'
Covered by: Gary Moore, Prince, John Lee Hooker

10 'BOLD AS LOVE'
Covered by: The Pretenders, John Mayer

LEGACY

BIOGRAPHIES

Billy Cox
(1941)

Jimi met bassist Cox in the army and they started The King Kasuals together in the early 1960s. Fast forward to 1969 and the friends reunited to form Band of Gypsys for a short-lived tour and live album.

Noel Redding
(1945–2003)

Redding originally auditioned for The Animals but Chas Chandler asked him to join Hendrix on bass instead. He quit the band in 1969, citing difficulties working with Jimi as well as the gruelling tour schedule.

Chas Chandler
(1938–96)

The former bassist for The Animals, Chandler raised the money to get Hendrix to London and introduced him to Eric Clapton. Chandler parted ways with Hendrix in 1969 because of musical and personal differences. He went on to manage Slade.

Roger Mayer

The electronic whizz who developed the Octavia pedal, Mayer introduced himself to Hendrix after a gig and the two embarked on a sonic journey that developed into a great friendship. Roger Mayer Guitar Effects are still in production.

Kathy Etchingham
(1946–)

British DJ and writer, Etchingham was just 20 years old when she met Hendrix in London in 1966. Etchingham was already part of the Swinging London scene and was friends with Eric Burdon, Brian Jones and Paul McCartney.

Keith Altham

Journalist Keith Altham interviewed Hendrix eight times and became a close friend. He recorded Hendrix's last interview at the Cumberland Hotel, five days before his death. Altham claims he told Hendrix to set fire to his guitar at the Monterey Pop Festival.

**Lithofayne Pridgon
(1940–)**
Party girl Pridgon was Hendrix's girlfriend in New York in 1963. She was possibly the inspiration for Hendrix's track 'Foxy Lady' as well as other songs such as 'Fire' and 'Love or Confusion' where he laments a lost love.

**Eric Burdon
(1941–)**
The lead singer for The Animals became a close friend of Hendrix through his friendship with Kathy Etchingham and association with Chas Chandler. Burdon played with Hendrix a few days before his death.

Gerry Stickells
Stickells was a roadie with The Jimi Hendrix Experience from November 1966 until Hendrix's death in 1970. After Hendrix's death, Gerry became the manager of the Electric Lady Studios in New York before setting up his own tour management company.

**Frank Michael
'Mike' Jeffery
(1933–73)**
Former manager of The Animals and co-manager with Chas Chandler of The Jimi Hendrix Experience, Jeffery died in a plane crash in 1973.

**Mitch
Mitchell
(1946–2008)**
Mitchell was the drummer on all three of The Jimi Hendrix Experience albums and performed at the Isle of Wight Festival in 1970. Mitchell died in Portland, Oregon, in 2008, days after completing a tour of the USA celebrating Hendrix's music.

**Monika
Dannemann
(1945–96)**
The German figure-skater was the last known person to be with Hendrix on the morning of his death. Dannemann claimed Hendrix had asked her to marry him, which conflicted with reports of them fighting. She committed suicide in 1996.

band member   manager

friend   lover

INDEX

'1983... (A Merman I Should Turn to Be)' 64, 65, 69, 72
27 Club, The 84–5

A
Ackerman, Toni 47
Acuff, Roy 38
'All Along the Watchtower' 69, 73, 83, 86
Altham, Keith 92
amps 78–9
animals, love of 39, 72–3
Animals, The 27
appearance 32–3, 46–7
Are You Experienced 10, 28, 29, 56–7, 78, 83
army career 9, 23, 48, 49
art, love of 39
Auerbach, Dan 80
Axis: Bold As Love 29, 62–3, 83

B
Band of Gypsys 70, 83, 92
Beatles, The 40, 42, 46
Beck, Jeff 40, 90
Berry, Chuck 23
birth 15
Blaises Club 40
Blue Flames 25
'Bold as Love' 63, 64, 65, 91
Braun, Michael 47
Breakaways, The 57
23 Brook Street 40, 86–7
Burdon, Eric 41, 80, 93
Burke, Solomon 24
'Burning of the Midnight Lamp' 29, 69
Burton, Trevor 63

C
Capitol Records 16
Carnaby Street 42–3
'Castles Made of Sand' 63, 64, 65
Chandler, Chas 10, 25, 41, 57, 60, 63, 92
Charles, Ray 38
Cherokee heritage 38
Clapton, Eric 10, 26, 42, 45, 78, 80
Cobain, Kurt 14, 52
Coeuroy, André 16
colour, love of 64–5
'Come On (Part 1)' 64, 69
Cooke, Sam 9, 25
covers of songs 90–1
Cox, Billy 24, 92
'Crosstown Traffic' 64, 65, 69, 91
Cumberland Hotel, The 41, 92

D
Dannemann, Monika 34, 93
death 34
decibel levels 50–1
drugs 31, 49
Dury, Ian 18
Dylan, Bob 27, 80

E
earnings 60–1
Eastman 68
Electric Ladyland 68–9, 83
Etchingham, Kathy 27, 31, 40, 41, 86, 92
eyesight 33

F
Faithfull, Marianne 41
family tree 20–1
'Fire' 57, 90, 93
First Rays of the New Rising Sun 83

'Foxy Lady' 29, 57, 73, 90, 93
Franklin, Aretha 18
Frusciante, John 81
Fuzz Face pedal 78

G
Garcia, Jerry 19
Gibb, Barry 42
Grant, Eddy 86
guitars and equipment 22, 23, 44, 58–9, 78–9
Gunterstone Road 40

H
Handel, George Frideric 86, 87
Harrison, George 86
Hayes, Isaac 19
Hendrix, Al 9, 15, 20, 23
Hendrix, Joseph 20
Hendrix, Leon 20
Hendrix, Lucille 9, 15, 20, 21, 22, 23
Hendrix, Zenora 20, 38
Hendrix chord, the 74
'Hey Joe' 8, 28, 29, 56, 57
'House Burning Down' 64, 65, 69, 72
Howlin' Wolf 9, 38

I
'If 6 Was 9' 63, 74
influence on music 80–1
influences on 38–9
Iommi, Tony 52
Isle of Wight Festival, 1970 10, 44, 67
Isley Brothers, The 9, 25, 81

J
Jagger, Chris 46
Jagger, Mick 42, 80
James, Elmore 9, 38
James, Tamika Laurice 21
Jeffrey, Mike 60, 93

Jimi Hendrix Experience, The 28, 40, 60, 61, 70–1, 83
Jones, Brian 10, 18, 69, 80
Jones, Tom 43

K
Keith, Linda 25
King, Albert 44, 52
King, B.B. 9, 25
King Kasuals, The 24
Klinghoffer, Josh 80
Kramer, Eddie 57, 63
Kravitz, Lenny 81

L
law infringements 48–9
left-handedness 32, 33, 52
Lennon, John 80
Little Richard 9, 25
'Little Wing' 63, 73, 90
live performances 60–1, 70–1
London 26–7, 40–3

M
McCartney, Paul 19, 52, 80
Malmsteen, Yngwie 81
'Manic Depression' 57, 90
Marr, Johnny 81
Marshall amps 78–9
Mayer, John 80
Mayer, Roger 56, 62, 78, 92
Mayfield, Curtis 19
Mercer, Johnny 16
Mitchell, Mitch 28, 57, 63, 69, 93
Money, Zoot 27, 40
Moon, Keith 40
Morello, Tom 9, 77, 80
Morgan, Huey 54
music in 1942 16–17

N
Nash, Graham 18
Neil, Simon 80

O
Octavia pedal 78
'One Rainy Wish' 63, 64, 65

P
People, Hell and Angels 83
Petrillo, James 16
poetry 39
Presley, Elvis 38
Pridgon, Lithofayne 93
'Purple Haze' 10, 28, 29, 65, 74, 78, 90

R
'Rainy Day, Dream Away' 69, 72
'Red House' 57, 64, 91
Redding, Noel 28, 57, 63, 69, 92
Redding, Otis 24
Reed, Lou 18
'Remember' 57, 65, 72, 73
Ronnie Scott's Jazz Club 41
Ross, Mike 57
Royal Albert Hall 17, 40

S
Samarkland Hotel 34, 41
Satriani, Joe 81
Scotch of St James 40
Shepherd, Kenny Wayne 81
'She's So Fine' 63, 72
shyness 30
Siddle, David 57
Slash 81
Smith, Robert 81
space travel 39
'Spanish Castle Magic' 63, 64, 73, 74
Star Spangled Rhythm 16
Starr, Ringo 41
Stephen, John 43
'Stepping Stone' 83
Stickells, Gerry 93
Summers, Andy 27, 40

Sundquist, James Henrik Daniel 21

T
temper 31
Townshend, Pete 13, 40, 78
TV appearance, first 82
Twiggy 43

U
Uni-Vibe pedal 78

V
Vai, Steve 81
'Valleys of Neptune' 64, 65, 72
Vaughan, Stevie Ray 81
voice, confidence about 31
'Voodoo Child (Slight Return)' 69, 91
'Voodoo Chile' 68, 69, 69, 74, 78

W
wah-wah pedal 78
'Wait Until Tomorrow' 63, 64
Waters, Muddy 9, 23, 38
White, Jack 80
Williams, Hank 38
Wilson, Brian 19
Wilson, Jackie 9, 25
'Wind Cries Mary, The' 28, 29, 57, 64, 65, 91
Winwood, Steve 69
Womack, Bobby 30
Woodstock Festival, 1969 10, 47, 48, 61, 66

Y
Young, Neil 81

Z
Zappa, Frank 78

MEMORABLE HENDRIX PERFORMANCES

ADMIT ONE | OLYMPIA THEATRE | OCTOBER
PARIS | 1966

★ MARCH 1968 ★
CAFE AU GO GO
NEW YORK

BERKELEY
COMMUNITY
THEATER
MAY 1970
CALIFORNIA

MONTEREY
POP FESTIVAL
JUNE 1967

ROYAL
ALBERT HALL
FEBRUARY
1969
· LONDON ·

L. A. FORUM
· APRIL 1970 ·

WINTERLAND BALLROOM
OCTOBER 1968
SAN FRANCISCO

ADMIT ONE | WOODSTOCK
AUGUST 1969
· NEW YORK ·

ISLE OF WIGHT
FESTIVAL
AUGUST 1970

FILLMORE EAST ·
NEW YORK ·
JANUARY 1970
WITH BAND
OF GYPSYS